Asia
Sahara Desert
Africa
Kenya
Lake Victoria
Mount Meru
Serengeti National Park
Arusha
Tanzania
I0821660

A SPEEDY LITTLE CHEETAH ON THE BIG BLUE EARTH

To Brooke, for your inspiration and to Rebecca, for your vision—the Big Blue Earth books have bloomed beyond anything I imagined.—T.C.

To Rebecca Glaser and Tory Christie, "Big Blue Earth" stewards. To Mary Thomas, my eyes on the savanna when I was illustrating this book. To Emilia, big cat love.—L.N.P.

Published in 2026 by Amicus Ink, an imprint of Amicus • P.O. Box 227 • Mankato, MN 56002 • www.amicuspublishing.us

Library of Congress Cataloging-in-Publication Data
Names: Christie, Tory author | Powell, Luciana Navarro illustrator
Title: A speedy little cheetah on the big blue earth / by Tory Christie ; illustrated by Luciana Navarro Powell.
Description: Mankato, Minnesota : Amicus Ink, 2026. | Series: Big blue earth | Audience term: Children | Audience: Ages 4–8 | Audience: Grades K–1 | Summary: "This illustrated poem illuminates a unique geographical perspective, showcasing the African savanna with ever-widening views from a speedy young cheetah to the planet in space. Includes a glossary and a labeled map of Africa"—Provided by publisher.
Identifiers: LCCN 2025013389 (print) | LCCN 2025013390 (ebook) |
ISBN 9798889880080 hardcover | ISBN 9798889880097 ebook
Subjects: CYAC: American poetry | Perspective (Philosophy)—Poetry |
Savanna animals—Poetry | Tanzania—Poetry | LCGFT: Poetry | Picture books
Classification: LCC PS3603.H7543 S67 2026 (print) | LCC PS3603.H7543 (ebook) |
DDC 811/.6—dc23/eng/20250430
LC record available at https://lccn.loc.gov/2025013389
LC ebook record available at https://lccn.loc.gov/2025013390

Editor: Rebecca Glaser | Designer: Kim Pfeffer

First edition 9 8 7 6 5 4 3 2 1

Printed in China

A SPEEDY LITTLE CHEETAH ON THE BIG BLUE EARTH

by Tory Christie

illustrated by Luciana Navarro Powell

A speedy little cheetah

Chases a gazelle

Leaping through wild, wispy grass

Swaying and stretching across the vast,
hot savanna

Around the farthest hill

Where a city bustles with markets

And motorcycles that
beep-beep-beep

At a jeep filled with rangers
in wide-brimmed hats

Rattling away onto
a bumpy road

Toward a hilly village

Surrounded by herds of impala
and wildebeest and zebra

Where stampeding hooves splish-splash-splish

through rains and muddy puddles

Year after year after year
in the Great Migration

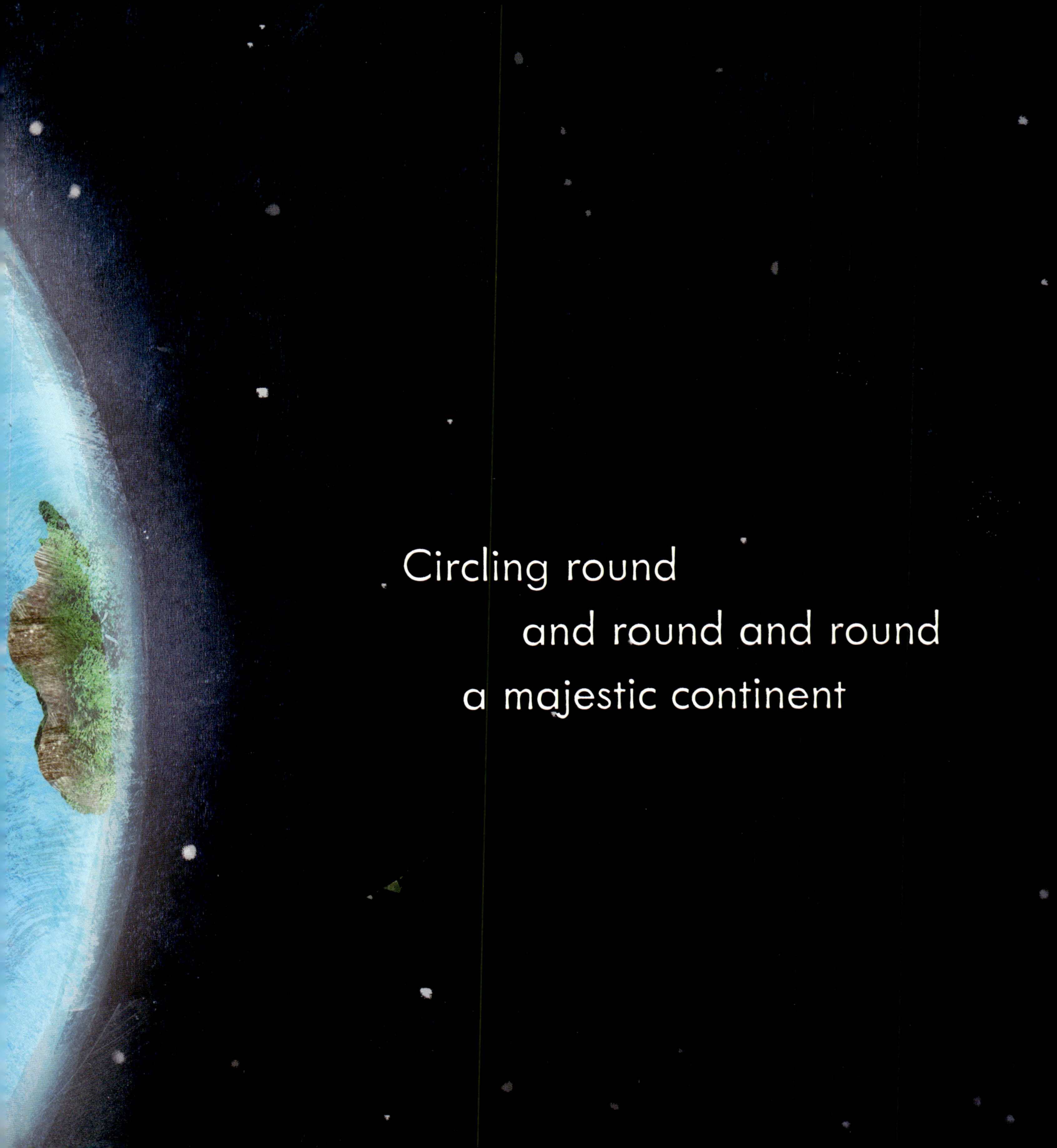

Circling round
and round and round
a majestic continent

On the big blue Earth…

...where a speedy
little cheetah
chases a gazelle.

AFRICA WORDS TO KNOW

Gazelles are small antelope known for graceful and swift movements. They jump with all four feet in the air. This is called pronking and may help them avoid predators.

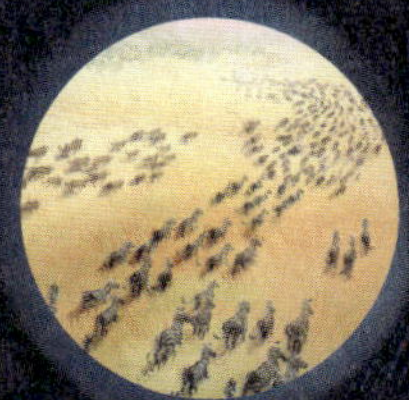

The **Great Migration** is the year-long movement of millions of wildebeest, zebra, gazelle, and other mammals around the eastern part of Africa, as they search for water.

Impalas are swift, medium-sized antelope with red glossy coats. Male impalas have long, twisted horns. Females don't have horns. Males and females usually travel in separate herds.

A **savanna** is a biome with grassy plains and few trees. On the savanna, rain only comes during one season, so animals move or migrate to find more water.

Wildebeests are horned animals that look like cattle except for their hairy beards and manes. They are the key players in the Great Migration. A wildebeest is sometimes called a gnu.

Atlantic
Ocean